W9-CFB-787

GAME DAY
Touchdown!
You Can Play Football

by Nick Fauchald

illustrated by Bill Dickson

Thanks to our advisers for their expertise, research, and advice:

Wendy Frappier, Ph.D.
Assistant Professor, Health and Physical Education Department
Minnesota State University
Moorhead, Minnesota

Susan Kesselring, M.A., Literacy Educator
Rosemount-Apple Valley-Eagan (Minnesota) School District

PICTURE WINDOW BOOKS
Minneapolis, Minnesota

Managing Editor: Bob Temple
Creative Director: Terri Foley
Editor: Brenda Haugen
Editorial Adviser: Andrea Cascardi
Copy Editor: Laurie Kahn
Designer: Nathan Gassman
Page production: Picture Window Books
The illustrations in this book are watercolor.

Picture Window Books
5115 Excelsior Boulevard
Suite 232
Minneapolis, MN 55416
1-877-845-8392
www.picturewindowbooks.com

Printed in the United States of America.

Library of Congress Cataloging-in-Publication Data
Fauchald, Nick.
Touchdown!: You can play football / written by Nick
Fauchald ; illustrated by Bill Dickson.
p. cm. — (Game day)
Summary: A brief introduction to the game of football as
intended to be played by children.
Includes bibliographical references (p.   ) and index.
ISBN 1-4048-0260-6 (lib. bdg.)
1. Football Juvenile literature. [1. Football.]
I. Dickson, Bill, 1949- ill. II. Title.
GV950.7 .F38 2004
796.332—dc22   2003019588

Football is as fun to play as it is to watch on TV. It's a game that includes a lot of running, kicking, and throwing. Two teams try to score points by throwing or carrying the ball past the other team's goal line or by kicking the ball through the other team's goalpost. The team with the most points wins.

You arrive at the field with your football and a bag full of gear. Your team, the Colts, is practicing throwing and catching.

The other team, the Bears, is doing jumping jacks and stretching their muscles.

To play football you need a helmet, pads, shoes with cleats, and a football. The game is played on a long field that is divided into yards. At each end of the field are a goal line, goalpost, and end zone. Each game is divided into four quarters.

5

When both teams are dressed and warmed up, they line up on the field. The referee tells both teams to have a good, fun game.

The referee tosses a coin in the air to see who chooses if they want the ball first. The Bears call, **"Heads!"** They guessed right, so they get to decide.

Each team has 11 players on the field at one time. The team with the ball is called the offense. The offense tries to move the ball toward the other team's goal line to score. The other team plays defense. The defense tries to keep the other team from crossing the goal line.

The Bears choose to receive the ball, so the Colts will kick off. All of the Colts line up behind Jesse, who kicks the ball high into the air toward the Bears.

The kicker places the ball on a rubber tee, runs toward the ball, and kicks the bottom half of it to make the ball fly high and far.

9

A Bears player catches the ball and runs forward toward the Colts' end zone, but the Colts stop her.

Now the Bears have four plays, called downs, to move the ball forward 10 yards. Each down is done when the Bear with the ball is tackled or runs out of bounds.

Professional teams tackle the player with the ball. You might only have to pull a flag off the offensive player's belt or tag him or her with two hands to stop the play.

The Bears line up on one side of the ball. The Colts line up on the other. The Bears' quarterback yells, "Down! Set! Hike!" The center snaps him the ball.

The place where the ball lies on the field at the beginning of a play is called the line of scrimmage. After getting the ball from the center, the quarterback leads the offense. The quarterback can pass, run, or hand the ball to another player.

The quarterback hands the ball to the running back, who runs five yards before Amanda tackles him. The Bears now have three downs left and five more yards to go.

The Bears fail to move the ball forward during the next two downs, so they decide to punt.

The kicker punts the ball toward the Colts, and Mario catches it. Mario runs past six Bears before they stop him!

On fourth down, teams often punt because it makes the other team start farther back. If the offense decides to try for a first down and gets stopped, the other team gets the ball at that spot.

15

Keri, the Colts' quarterback, calls the play.
The center snaps the ball.

Keri throws the ball to Ross, who catches it and runs for 13 yards. **First down!**

To throw a football, grip the ball with your fingertips across the top of the laces. Bring the ball back behind your ear, and snap it forward so it spins as much as possible. This is called a spiral and helps the ball fly straight.

You line up as a running back.

The center snaps the ball to Keri.

When catching a ball that is thrown high, put your thumbs and index fingers together so they make a diamond. When the ball hits your hands, pull the ball into your chest, and tuck it underneath your arm before running. If the ball is thrown low, scoop the ball with your pinkies together.

You run to the right, and Keri flips the ball to you.
You catch it and head up the field.

There are only two Bears between you and the end zone. You dodge the first Bear and jump over the second as he dives at your feet. You scamper into the end zone.

Touchdown! The Colts are ahead, 6-0, but there are three more quarters of football to play.

After a touchdown, a team can try to score an extra point by kicking the ball through the goalpost. The team can choose to try for two points by lining up near the goal line and trying to run or pass the ball into the end zone again.

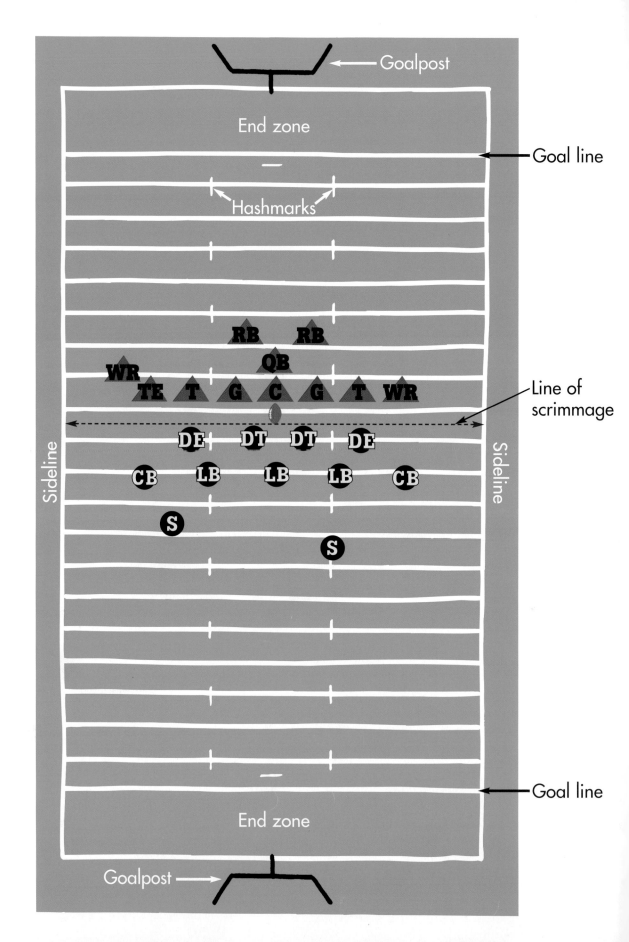

Key: Football Positions

▲ Offense

RB	Running back
QB	Quarterback
C	Center
G	Guard
T	Tackle
TE	Tight end
WR	Wide receiver

● Defense

DT	Defensive tackle
DE	Defensive end
LB	Linebacker
CB	Cornerback
S	Safety

Fun Facts

 The first Super Bowl was played in 1967. The Green Bay Packers defeated the Kansas City Chiefs, 35-10.

 The first professional football league was formed in 1920. It was called the American Professional Football Association. In 1922, it changed its name to the National Football League (NFL).

 Footballs used to be made out of pigskin. Now they are made from other materials.

 Football was inspired by soccer and rugby.

 The first official rules for football were written in 1876. A touchdown was worth four points, and a field goal was worth five points.

 Gary Anderson is the NFL's all-time leading scorer. He scored more than 2,200 points in his career as a kicker.

Glossary

center—the person who snaps the ball to the quarterback to start a play

defense—the team trying to stop the other team from scoring

down—a play in football. A team gets four downs, or chances, to move the football forward 10 yards.

line of scrimmage—the imaginary line across a football field that goes out from where the football lies before a play begins

offense—the team that has the ball

punt—to kick the ball to the other team when you have not been able to gain 10 yards in three downs

tackle—to knock or pull a person to the ground

To Learn More

At the Library

Brooks, Walter R. *Freddy Plays Football.* New York: Overlook Press, 2001.

Buckley, James. *Football.* New York: DK Pub., 1999.

Gibbons, Gail. *My Football Book.* New York: HarperCollins Publishers, 2000.

Goin, Kenn. *Football For Fun.* Minneapolis. Compass Point Books, 2003.

Kessler, Leonard. *Kick, Pass, and Run.* New York: HarperCollins, 1996.

On the Web

Fact Hound
Fact Hound offers a safe, fun way to find Web sites related to this book.
All of the sites on Fact Hound have been researched by our staff.
http://www.facthound.com

1. Visit the Fact Hound home page.
2. Enter a search word related to this
   book, or type in this special code:1404802606.
3. Click on the FETCH IT button.

Your trusty Fact Hound will fetch the best sites for you!

Index